Monterrey Medallions

D0128577

¡Bienvenidos Amigos!

This winter, I travelled to Mexico for the International Quilt Guild of Monterrey's annual seminar. I was welcomed by a diverse and fun-loving group of quilters. Some have lived in Mexico for years, while others were brand new to the country. These women have found many creative and resourceful ways to adjust to their new life in Mexico, so it was not surprising that they found so many different ways to interpret the medallion quilt! One idea led to the next and the next . . . and in the end, no two quilts looked alike.

Whether you choose the Simple or Challenge version of this quilt, you can arrange your blocks any way you'd like. Follow the layouts given or take off on your own "Mexican adventure" . . . either way, your destination will include a wonderful quilt. **¡Hasta luego!**

CONTENTS

Atkinson Designs • 19160 Zane St. • Elk River, MN 55330 • 763-441-1825 • fax 763-441-7288 • atkinsondesigns.com

Atkinson Designs

19160 Zane Street NW
Elk River, MN 55330

Tel: **763-441-1825**
Fax: **763-441-7288**

www.atkinsondesigns.com

Credits

Photography . . . . Altobell Imagery, St. Cloud, MN

Photo Set Design . . . . . . Liz Lois, Salem, WI

Graphic Design . . . . Vicki Higgins, Rogers, MN

Machine Quilting . . . . . . Lynn Rodby, Cindy Kujawa, Leona Orendorff

Acknowledgements

Lisa Bergeson and SanDee Cottell for their warm hospitality and their hard work setting up the seminar in Monterrey.

The International Quilt Guild of Monterrey Mexico for testing the medallion quilt at their annual seminar. Their creativity was truly an inspiration!

Lynn Rodby, Trish Polgreen, and Susie Lenz for sewing and pattern testing.

The shops in the Wild West Shop Hop for sharing feedback on yardage, color, etc.

Megan Atkinson, for giving up her room during the photo shoot.

Derek Atkinson, for his fluency in Spanish.

Kirk Atkinson (and everyone who has called to comment on our spelling) - there really is an extra "R" in Monterrey, Mexico.

Copyright 2005 Terry Atkinson

FABRIC REQUIREMENTS

- Finished quilt sizes: **Square:** 72" x 72" **Twin:** 72" x 90" **Queen:** 90" x 90"
- Numbers in parentheses are for the three sizes: (square, twin, queen) Take a moment before you begin to circle or highlight the numbers for the size you wish to make. For example, circle the center number if you are making the twin size. (21, ⟨26⟩ 32)
- Choose the "Simple" or "Challenge" version of this medallion quilt.
- For a scrappy background, simply use ½ yd. cuts instead of the background yardage.
- If you'd like to use fewer prints, substitute one ½ yd. for every two fat quarters.
- If you'd like to use more prints, assorted scraps may be substituted for the fat quarters.

SIMPLE QUILT

- Shown on pages 11 and 13.
- A confident beginner with an accurate seam allowance will enjoy making this easier version of the medallion quilt.
- Use prints that contrast well with your background fabric.

Background ($2^7/8$, $3^3/4$, $5^1/4$) yds.

Assorted Prints (21, 26, 32) fat quarters (18" x 21")

Binding ($5/8$, $3/4$, $3/4$) yd.

Backing ($4^1/2$, $5^1/2$, $8^1/4$) yds.

CHALLENGE QUILT

- Shown on the front and back covers and page 14.
- Triangles and contrast squares have been added to make this version more detailed and more challenging to sew.
- The contrast should be a solid or tone on tone that stands out from both the background and the prints.

Background ($3^1/2$, $4^1/2$, 6) yds.

Contrast ($1^1/8$, $1^1/4$, $1^1/4$) yds.

Assorted Prints (16, 20, 25) fat quarters (18" x 21")

Binding ($5/8$, $3/4$, $3/4$) yd.

Backing ($4^1/2$, $5^1/2$, $8^1/4$) yds.

CENTER STAR

Use several prints for this simple star.
Turn to **page 6** for instructions.

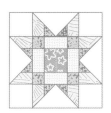

CENTER STAR

Add a contrast and some background triangles for a dynamic star.
Turn to **page 16** for instructions.

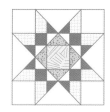

WOODPILE

These blocks surround the center star.
Turn to **page 7** for instructions.

WOODPILE

Contrast squares form a chain within these blocks.
Turn to **page 17** for instructions.

FLOATING STARS

The floating points make these stars turn out perfect every time.
Turn to **page 8** for instructions.

FLOATING STARS

Use one print for each star or mix and match prints for scrappy stars.
Turn to **page 18** for instructions.

FOUR PATCH CHAIN

Background squares make a simple chain in these border blocks.
Turn to **page 9** for instructions.

JACOB'S LADDER

Contrast squares are surrounded by background triangles to make a chain.
Turn to **page 19** for instructions.

FABRIC SELECTION FOR SCRAPPY QUILTS

When choosing fabrics, arrange them on a table so that just a little bit of each one shows, in about the same proportion as you'll see in the quilt. Add some background, then step back and take a look.

First, eliminate any that do not contrast enough with the background.

Second, look for any fabric that really stands out. Eliminate it or add a few more "standouts" for balance.

Third, check to make sure you have enough variety. The fabrics should look interesting from a distance, with some smaller details to notice up close. Remember, they won't all be next to each other, so they don't have to "match"!

Did you include...
~ "nothing" prints or tone-on-tone prints
~ "spotty" prints
~ florals - several sizes
~ geometrics
~ plaids/stripes/checks
~ conversation prints
~ a few "off" colors
~ a few that are "too dark" or "too light"

Arrange your fabric by color "family", such as reds, blues, etc.

Do you have uneven amounts of color?
~ Papa Bear: use lots of this color
~ Mama Bear: use some of this color
~ Baby Bear: use just a little bit of this color

Next, rearrange the fabrics from light to dark, ignoring the color. Fill in any missing values. I find that I often have too many "mediums" and have to be sure to include some lighter & darker prints.

FABRIC PREPARATION

Use 100% cotton quilt shop quality fabrics for best results! Steam press all fabric before you begin.

You need 40" of useable fabric from 42" strips, and 20" of useable fabric from 21" strips.

CUTTING

Instructions given are for rotary cutting. Measurements include 1/4" seam allowance.

First Cut: Square the fabric edge, and cut strips across the width of the fabric from selvedge to selvedge. Strips will be about 40" - 42" long.

Second Cut: Turn the strips and square the end. Crosscut pieces from the strips.

SEAM ALLOWANCE

All seams are 1/4". Test your 1/4" seam allowance before you begin!! Cut three scraps 1 1/2" x 3 1/2". Stitch them together along the long edges and press. The resulting square should measure exactly 3 1/2" x 3 1/2"!

FOLDED CORNERS

Mark: On the wrong side of a small square, mark a diagonal line from corner to corner with a crease or light pencil mark.

Stitch: Place the small square on top of the rectangle, right sides together. Stitch on the marked line. When chain-piecing, stop with the needle down between pieces, so that you can start sewing with the next corner right up against the needle. Lift the presser foot between pieces, so they don't get pushed out of alignment.

Press & Trim: Fold the corner up and press. From the wrong side, trim the layers in the corner even with the edges of the rectangle. (If you sewed exactly on the line there won't be anything to trim, but who is perfect every time?) To reduce bulk, trim the underneath layers to 1/4".

To avoid marking all those squares, just mark your machine! Put the needle down and slide a ruler up against the needle. Lower the presser foot to hold the ruler in place, and draw a line with a permanent marker straight out from the needle. When sewing a folded corner, the corners will line up with the needle and the line! As you stitch, watch the corner travel up the line instead of watching the needle.

machine needle

line on machine

PRESSING

Press in the direction shown by the arrows.
When there are no arrows shown, you can press either
way, or follow. . .

" Rules for Pressing"

~ Press toward the dark fabric. This prevents the dark
  fabric from "shadowing" through to the front.
~ Press seams in opposite directions. This will help you
  get nice sharp corners without pinning!
~ Press in the least bulky direction. If there is a point
  along the outside edge that will be crossed by another
  seam, press away from that point.
~ If all else fails, press it whichever way it wants to go!!

Remember, rules are made to be broken!
There's no way to follow all of these rules at the same
time! You'll have to use your good judgement. It's okay
to press bulky seams open, or press part of a seam one
way and part the other way to reduce bulk.

To Steam or not to Steam . . .

Some quilters use a dry iron because they feel that
steam stretches the fabric . . . but I like steam because
it makes a nice crease with just one touch of the iron.
Without steam, I find myself pushing and rubbing with
the iron to flatten the fabric, which ends up stretching
it even more!

PINNING

My favorite method of pinning is to skip it! However, for
those times when you can't avoid it, be sure to use fine
silk pins for the most accurate results.
**Before pinning, check to be sure that all of your
points are ¹/₄" in from the edge of the block.** Poke a
pin into the fabric ¹/₄" from the edge (right where you'll be
stitching) through the points on both layers. Leave it
sticking straight up, and insert two "helper" pins - one on
each side of the "poker" pin. **Remember:** If you tilt the
"poker," your points will move and won't match! Remove
the "poker" pin before sewing.

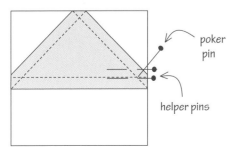

poker
pin

helper pins

BINDING

Note: These steps are the same regardless of the
corner angle.
Prepare Binding: Join the binding strips as shown. Trim
seams to ¹/₄" and press open. Press one end of the
binding at a 45 angle and trim to ¹/₄". Fold the binding in
half lengthwise, with wrong sides together, and press.

Prepare Quilt: Trim quilt edges with rotary cutter.
Hand baste along the edges if needed to keep layers
from shifting.

Stitch Binding To Quilt:

On the right side of the
quilt, stitch the binding to
the edge (with raw edges
even) using a ¹/₄" seam.
Stop ¹/₄" from the corner
and backstitch. Remove
quilt from the machine.

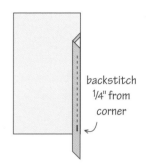

backstitch
¹/₄" from
corner

Turn the quilt and fold the binding up, and then down
along the next edge of the quilt. A little pleat will form
at the corner. Stitch the binding to the second side of
the quilt, stopping ¹/₄" from the corner, and backstitch.

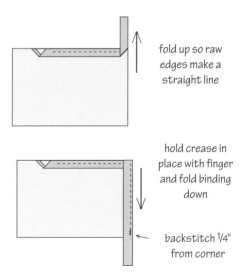

fold up so raw
edges make a
straight line

hold crease in
place with finger
and fold binding
down

backstitch ¹/₄"
from corner

Repeat these steps until you reach the
starting point. Cut the binding off at an
angle and tuck the end into the fold. Fold
the binding around the edge of the quilt to
the back, and stitch in place by hand.

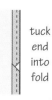

tuck
end
into
fold

Cut pieces from the assorted print fat quarters.

CUTTING (same for all sizes)

FIRST CUT	SECOND CUT
Background cut 2 strips 5" x 42"	cut 4 - 5" x 9½"
	cut 4 - 5" x 5"
Print (points) cut 2 strips 2¾" x 21"	
Print (high contrast) cut 2 - 2¾" x 21" cut 4 - 2¾" x 2¾"	
Print (rectangles) cut 4 - 2¾" x 5"	
Print (center square) cut one 5" x 5"	

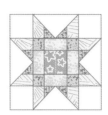

TERRY'S TIP

When choosing prints for this block, overlap them as shown below, arranging them in order from the center square out to the background. The high contrast print should really stand out! Choose a variety of prints and values so they do not blend together.

center print

background

SEWING (same for all sizes)

A. Arrange 2¾" print squares and 2¾" x 5" print rectangles around the 5" center square as shown. Stitch into rows, pressing seams in the direction shown by the arrows.

Stitch the rows together, pressing the seams away from the center. **Square should measure 9½" x 9½".**

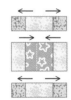

B. Stitch the 2¾" x 21" print and high contrast print strips together as shown. Press seams toward contrast. **Strip sets must measure 5" x 21".** Cut eight 5" units.

cut 8

5"   sew 2 sets

2¾" x 21" high contrast
2¾" x 21" print

C. Place a Step B unit on each 5" x 9½" background rectangle **exactly** as shown. Mark a diagonal line on the Step B unit and stitch on the line. Press and trim seams to ¼".

mark   stitch   press & trim

make 4

D. Repeat on the opposite end **exactly** as shown.

mark   stitch   press & trim

make 4

E. Arrange Step D units and 5" background squares around the Step A square as shown. Stitch into rows, pressing seams in the direction shown by the arrows.

Stitch the rows together, pressing the seams away from the center. **Block should measure 18½" x 18½".**

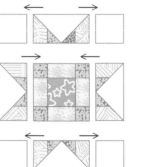 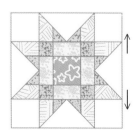

CUTTING (same for all sizes)

FIRST CUT	SECOND CUT

Background

cut 1 strip 8" x 42"........cut 2 - 8" x 21"
cut 1 strip 6½" x 42".....cut 2 - 6½" x 21"
cut 1 strip 5" x 42"........cut 2 - 5" x 21"
cut 1 strip 3½" x 42".....cut 2 - 3½" x 21"
cut 1 strip 2" x 42"........cut 2 - 2" x 21"

Assorted Prints

cut 2 - 8" x 21"
cut 2 - 6½" x 21"
cut 2 - 5" x 21"
cut 2 - 3½" x 21"
cut 2 - 2" x 21"
cut 20 - 2 x 9½"

TERRY'S TIP

Choose prints that are similar in value that contrast well with the background. Use a variety of prints for the 2 x 9½" strips and the blocks will be easy to arrange.

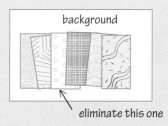

background

eliminate this one

SEWING (same for both sizes)

A. BEFORE YOU BEGIN: **Test your seam allowance! If it is not exact, your blocks will not be square!** Refer to "Before you Begin" on page 4) Stitch the assorted print strips and background strips into sets exactly as shown. Make two sets of each. Press all seams toward the print. **Strip sets must measure 9½" x 21".** Cut each set into 2" units.

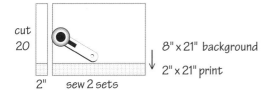

cut 20

2"   sew 2 sets

8" x 21" background
2" x 21" print

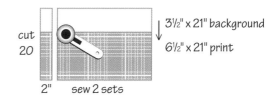

cut 20

2"   sew 2 sets

3½" x 21" background
6½" x 21" print

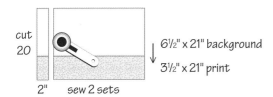

cut 20

2"   sew 2 sets

6½" x 21" background
3½" x 21" print

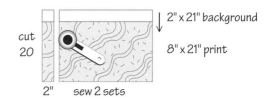

cut 20

2"   sew 2 sets

2" x 21" background
8" x 21" print

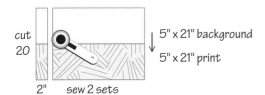

cut 20

2"   sew 2 sets

5" x 21" background
5" x 21" print

B. Stitch Step A units and the 2 x 9½" print rectangles together **exactly** as shown to make 8 blocks and 12 reverse blocks. Press as shown by the arrow. **Blocks must measure 9½" x 9½".**

make 8

make 12 reverse

FLOATING STARS, simple version

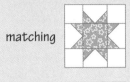
TERRY'S TIP

✂ CUTTING (Square, Twin, Queen)

FIRST CUT	SECOND CUT

Background
cut (5, 9, 15) strips 4½" x 42" . . . cut (48, 96, 160) 3½" x 4½"
cut (5, 9, 15) strips 3½" x 42" . . . cut (48, 96, 160) 3½" x 3½"

Assorted Prints
Cut 1 or 2 stars from each print for a total of (12, 24, 40) stars.

for one star:
cut 1 strip 5" x 21" . . . . cut 8 - 2½" x 2½"
                                             cut 1 - 4½" x 4½"

open and cut this
from single layer

for two stars:
cut 1 strip 5" x 21" . . . . cut 8 - 2½" x 2½"
                                             cut 2 - 4½" x 4½"
cut 1 strip 2½" x 21". . . . . cut 8 - 2½" x 2½"

How will you arrange the prints in
your stars?

matching

contrasting

scrappy

✎ SEWING (Square, Twin, Queen)

Repeat Steps A - C to make (12, 24, 40) blocks.

	BACKGROUND	PRINT
PIECES FOR ONE STAR:	4 - 3½" x 4½"	8 - 2½" x 2½"
	4 - 3½" x 3½"	1 - 4½" x 4½"

A. Mark a diagonal line on the wrong side of eight 2½"
print squares. Place a marked square on the corner of
four 3½" x 4½" background rectangles **exactly as
shown**. Stitch on the line. Trim corner, leaving ¼" seam
allowance. Press toward corner.

mark using
pencil
or chalk

stitch

trim

make 4
press

Repeat on the
adjacent corner.

make 4

triangles will overlap
¼" in from the edge

B. Arrange the Step A units around a 4½" print square
as shown. Place 3½" background squares at the
corners. Stitch into rows, pressing in the direction
shown by the arrows. Stitch the rows together. Press.

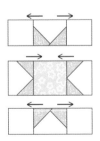

C. Spray the block lightly with Magic
Sizing® and press. **Trim block
to 9½" x 9½"**, trimming evenly
from all edges. (Trim about ¾"
over from the star points.)

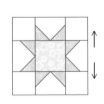
9½" x 9½"

Repeat Steps A - C to make (12, 24, 40) blocks.

FOUR PATCH CHAIN, *simple version*

CUTTING (Square, Twin, Queen)

TERRY'S TIP

Accuracy is very important for these blocks because they are along the edge of the quilt.

The cutting chart allows five 3½" x 3½" squares per 3½" x 21" strip. This allows for trimming the selvedges and squaring the end of the strips. If your strips are a little longer, you might get six squares from each strip.

FIRST CUT	SECOND CUT
Background	
cut (9, 10, 11) strips 2" x 42".	cut (17, 20, 22) 2" x 21"
Assorted Prints	
cut (34, 39, 44) strips 3½" x 21".	cut (168, 192, 216) 3½" x 3½"
cut (17, 20, 22) 2" x 21"	

SEWING (Square, Twin, Queen)

A. Stitch the 2" x 21" background and print strips into sets as shown. Press seams toward print. **Strip sets must measure 3½" x 21".** Cut into 2" units.

cut
(168, 192, 216)

2" x 21" background
2" x 21" print

2"   sew (17, 20, 22) sets

B. Stitch Step A units into pairs in a variety of combinations as shown. Press. **Squares must measure 3½" x 3½".**

make
(84, 96, 108)

TERRY'S TIP
The Step B squares must be **exactly** the same size as the 3½" print squares!

C. Arrange Step B squares and 3½" print squares as shown. Stitch into rows, pressing seams as shown by the arrows.

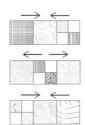

D. Stitch rows together, pressing seams away from center. **Blocks must measure 9½" x 9½".**

make (28, 32, 36)

OPTIONAL RAIL FENCE BLOCKS
These blocks are shown in the inside medallion corners of the batik quilt on page 14.

For four blocks, you'll need 12 - 2" x 21" print strips.

Stitch the 2" x 21" print strips into sets as shown. Press. **Strip sets must measure 9½" x 21".** Cut into 9½" squares.

cut
4

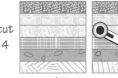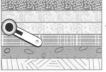

six strips
2" x 21" print

9½"   sew 2 sets

A. Mark the 12 Reverse woodpile blocks with a pin or a piece of tape to keep them from getting mixed up with the 8 regular blocks.

 8 blocks

B. Arrange the woodpile blocks and reverse woodpile blocks around the center star as shown. Follow the diagrams below or create your own layout!
Note: The reverse blocks are marked with "R".

 12 reverse blocks

C. Fill in around the woodpile blocks with star blocks.

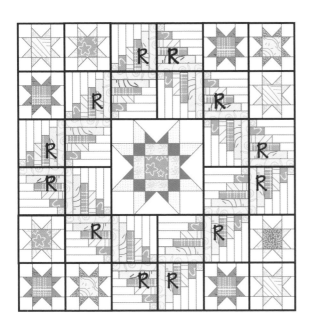

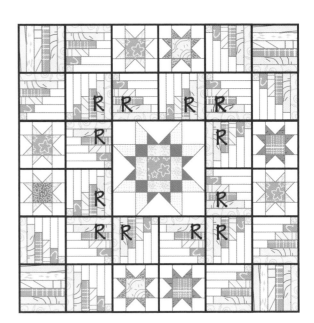

The optional Rail Fence blocks (page 9) have been used in the corners of these two settings. (You'll have four leftover star or woodpile blocks.)

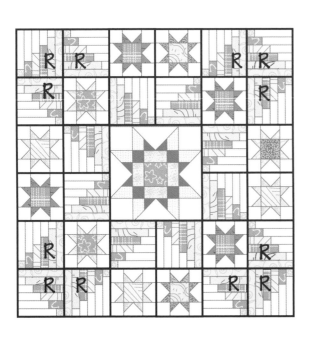

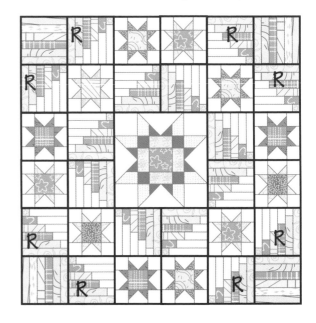

Monterrey Medallion, simple version

Don't Fence Me In

Monterrey Medallion, simple version

Monterrey Medallion, challenge version

A. Arrange the blocks in your desired setting. Stitch them into rows. Press seams in alternate directions. Stitch the rows together and press.

Square size is shown at right.

Twin size has an extra row of stars above and below the center section.

Queen size has an additional row of stars along the sides too.

B. Layer and quilt by hand or machine. Bind using (8, 9, 10) 2½" x 42" strips.

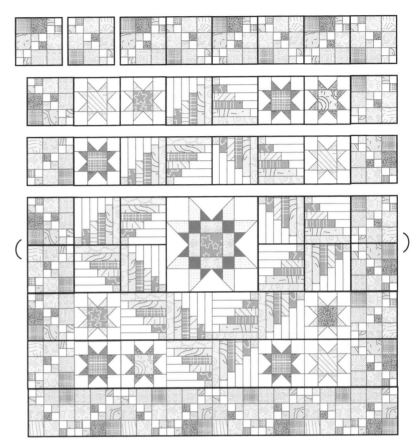

Square Size: 72" x 72"

Twin Size: 72" x 90"

Queen Size: 90" x 90"

CENTER STAR, challenge version

CUTTING (same for all sizes)

FIRST CUT	SECOND CUT
Background	
cut 2 strips 5" x 42"......	cut 4 - 5" x 9½"
	cut 4 - 5" x 5"
trim strip to 2¾".........	cut 8 - 2¾" x 2¾"
Contrast	
cut 2 strips 2¾" x 42"....	cut 2 - 2¾" x 21"
	cut 4 - 2¾" x 2¾"
Print (points)	
cut 2 strips 2¾" x 21"	
Print (large triangles)	
cut 4 - 2¾" x 5"	
Print (Center square)	
cut one 5" x 5"	

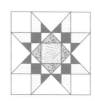

TERRY'S TIP

The contrast and point prints must contrast with the background **and** each other.

The center square and large triangle prints may blend into each other or contrast from each other - you'll get a pleasing effect either way.

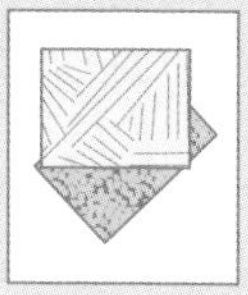

SEWING (same for all sizes)

A. Mark a diagonal line on the wrong side of the eight 2¾" background squares. Place a marked square on each of the four 2¾" x 5" print rectangles as shown. Stitch on the line. Press and trim seams to ¼". Repeat on the adjacent corner, using the remaining marked squares.

stitch   press   repeat   make 4

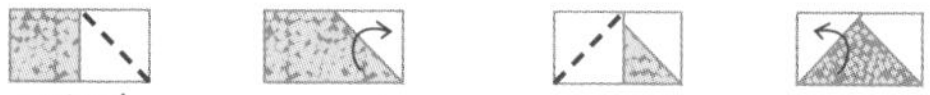

B. Arrange Step A units and 2¾" contrast squares around the 5" print square as shown. Stitch into rows, pressing seams in the direction shown by the arrows.

Stitch the rows together, pressing the seams away from the center. **Square should measure 9½" x 9½".**

All points should be ¼" in from the edge!

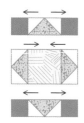

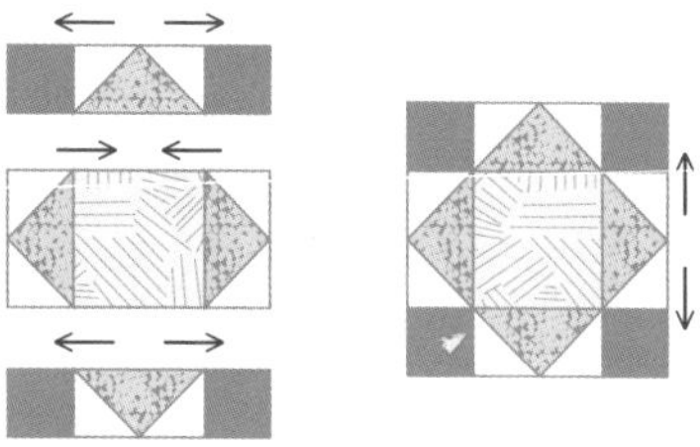

C. Stitch the 2¾" x 21" print and contrast strips together as shown. Press seams toward contrast. **Strip sets must measure 5" x 21".** Cut eight 5" units.

cut 8
5"   sew 2 sets
2¾" x 21" contrast
2¾" x 21" print

D. Place a Step C unit on each 5" x 9½" background rectangle **exactly** as shown. Mark a diagonal line on the Step C unit and stitch on the line. Press and trim seams to ¼".

mark   stitch   press & trim   make 4

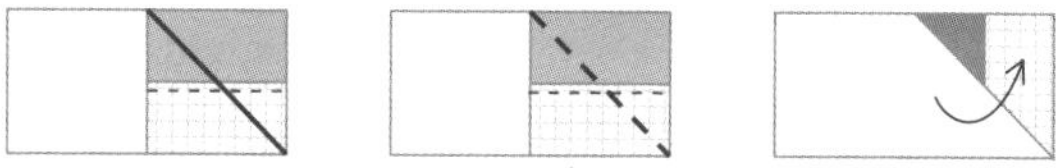

E. Repeat on the opposite end **exactly** as shown.

mark   stitch   press & trim   make 4

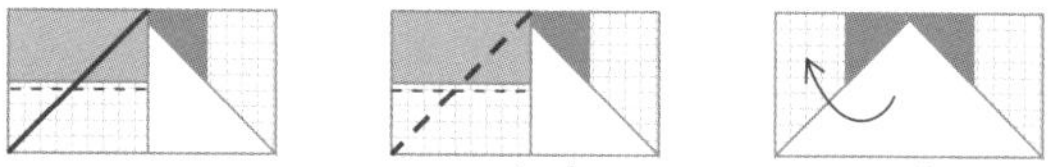

F. Arrange Step E units and 5" background squares around the Step B square as shown. Stitch into rows, pressing seams in the direction shown by the arrows.

Stitch the rows together, pressing the seams away from the center. **Block should measure 18½" x 18½".**

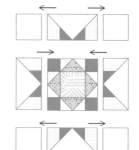 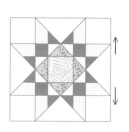

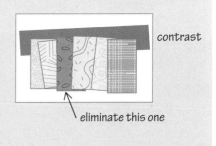

contrast

eliminate this one

CUTTING (same for all sizes)

FIRST CUT	SECOND CUT

Background
cut 1 strip 8" x 42"........cut 2 - 8" x 21"
cut 1 strip 6½" x 42"......cut 2 - 6½" x 21"
cut 1 strip 5" x 42".......cut 2 - 5" x 21"
cut 1 strip 3½" x 42"......cut 2 - 3½" x 21"
cut 1 strip 2" x 42".......cut 2 - 2" x 21"

Contrast
cut 6 strips 2" x 42".....cut 10 - 2" x 21"
                           cut 4 - 2" x 10½"

Assorted Prints
cut 4 - 8" x 10½"
cut 2 - 6½" x 21"
cut 2 - 5" x 21"
cut 2 - 3½" x 21"
cut 2 - 2" x 21"

SEWING (same for all sizes)

A. **Test your seam allowance before you begin** - seams must be perfect or your blocks will not be square! (See page 4) Stitch the assorted print strips, background strips, and contrast strips into sets exactly as shown. Make two sets of each. Press all seams toward contrast. **Strip sets must measure 9½" x 21".** Cut each set into 2" units.

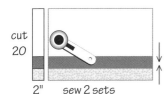

cut 20

2"   sew 2 sets

8" x 21" bkgrnd.
2" x 21" contrast

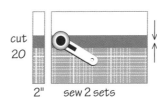

cut 20

2"   sew 2 sets

3½" x 21" bkgrnd.
2" x 21" contrast
5" x 21" print

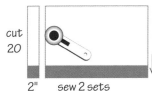

cut 20

2"   sew 2 sets

6½" x 21" bkgrnd.
2" x 21" contrast
2" x 21" print

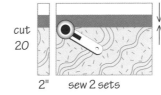

cut 20

2"   sew 2 sets

2" x 21" bkgrnd.
2" x 21" contrast
6½" x 21" print

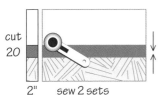

cut 20

2"   sew 2 sets

5" x 21" bkgrnd.
2" x 21" contrast
3½" x 21" print

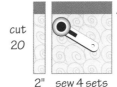

cut 20

2"   sew 4 sets

2" x 10½" contrast
8" x 10½" print

B. Stitch Step A units together **exactly** as shown to make 8 blocks and 12 reverse blocks. Press as shown by the arrows. **Blocks must measure 9½" x 9½".**

make 8

make 12 reverse

FLOATING STARS, challenge version

 CUTTING (Square, Twin, Queen)

TERRY'S TIP

How will you arrange the prints in your stars?

matching

contrasting

scrappy

FIRST CUT	SECOND CUT

Background
cut (5, 9, 15) strips 4½" x 42" ... cut (48, 96, 160) 3½" x 4½"
cut (5, 9, 15) strips 3½" x 42" ... cut (48, 96, 160) 3½" x 3½"

Assorted Prints
Cut 1 or 2 stars from each print for a total of (12, 24, 40) stars.

for one star:
cut 1 strip 5" x 21" . . . . cut 8 - 2½" x 2½"
cut 1 - 4½" x 4½"

open and cut this
from single layer

for two stars:
cut 1 strip 5" x 21" . . . . cut 8 - 2½" x 2½"
cut 2 - 4½" x 4½"
cut 1 strip 2½" x 21" . . . . cut 8 - 2½" x 2½"

SEWING (Square, Twin, Queen)

Repeat Steps A - C to make (12, 24, 40) blocks.

PIECES FOR ONE STAR:	BACKGROUND	PRINT
	4 - 3½" x 4½"	8 - 2½" x 2½"
	4 - 3½" x 3½"	1 - 4½" x 4½"

A. Mark a diagonal line on the wrong side of eight 2½" print squares. Place a marked square on the corner of **four** 3½" x 4½" background rectangles **exactly as shown**. Stitch on the line. Trim corner, leaving ¼" seam allowance. Press toward corner.

mark using pencil or chalk   stitch   trim   press

make 4

Repeat on the adjacent corner.

triangles will overlap ¼" in from the edge

make 4

B. Arrange the Step A units around a 4½" print square as shown. Place 3½" background squares at the corners. Stitch into rows, pressing in the direction shown by the arrows. Stitch the rows together. Press.

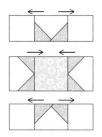

C. Spray the block lightly with Magic Sizing® and press. **Trim block to 9½" x 9½"**, trimming evenly from all edges. (Trim about ¾" over from the star points.)

9½" x 9½"

Repeat Steps A - C to make (12, 24, 40) blocks.

18

CUTTING (Square, Twin, Queen)

FIRST CUT	SECOND CUT
Background	
cut (6, 7, 8) strips 4" x 42"........	cut (56, 64, 72) 4" x 4"
cut (9, 10, 11) strips 2" x 42".......	cut (17, 20, 22) 2" x 21"
Contrast	
cut (9, 10, 11) strips 2" x 42"........	cut (17, 20, 22) 2" x 21"
Assorted Prints	
cut (12, 13, 15) strips 4" x 21"	cut (56, 64, 72) 4" x 4"
cut (12, 13, 15) strips 3½" x 21".....	cut (56, 64, 72) 3½" x 3½"

SEWING (Square, Twin, Queen)

A. Mark a diagonal line on the wrong side of the 4" background squares.

 mark using pencil or chalk

Place the marked squares on the 4" print squares with edges even and right sides together.

 layer

Stitch a **scant** ¼" from the line on both sides of the line as shown.

 stitch

Cut on the line. Press seams toward print.

cut   press

B. **Trim squares to 3½" x 3½".**

 trim

C. Stitch the 2" x 21" background and contrast strips into sets as shown. Press seams toward contrast. **Strip sets must measure 3½" x 21".** Cut into 2" units.

cut (168, 192, 216)   2" sew (17, 20, 22) sets

↓ 2" x 21" background
↓ 2" x 21" contrast

D. Stitch Step C units together into pairs as shown. Press. **Squares should measure 3½" x 3½".**

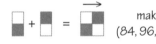 make (84, 96, 108)

E. Arrange the Step B and D squares and 3½" print squares as shown. Stitch into rows, pressing seams away from the triangles.

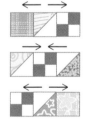

F. Stitch rows together, pressing seams away from center.

make (28, 32, 36)

DESIGN YOUR OWN SETTING, challenge version

A. Mark the 12 Reverse woodpile blocks with a pin or a piece of tape to keep them from getting mixed up with the 8 regular blocks.

B. Arrange the blocks and reverse blocks around the center star as shown. Follow the diagrams below or create your own layout!
Note: The reverse blocks are marked with "R".

C. Fill in around the woodpile blocks with star blocks.

8 blocks

12 reverse "R"

TERRY'S TIP

Your blocks can be arranged in many different ways. Experiment with several different settings before you decide - you might even come up with an original layout!

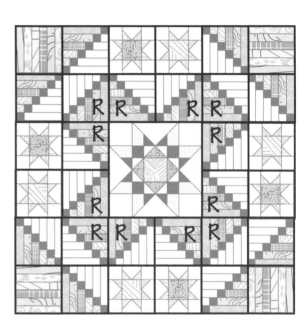

The optional Rail Fence blocks (page 9) have been used in the corners of these two settings. (You'll have four leftover star or woodpile blocks.)

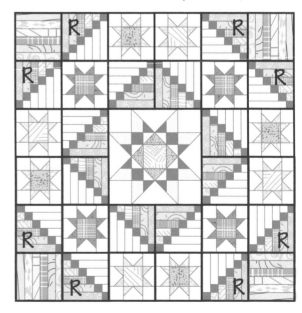

A. Arrange the blocks in your desired setting. Stitch them into rows. Press seams in alternate directions. Stitch the rows together and press.

Square size is shown at right.

Twin size has an extra row of stars above and below the center section.

Queen size has an additional row of stars along the sides too.

B. Layer and quilt by hand or machine. Bind using (8, 9, 10) 2½" x 42" strips.

Square Size: 72" x 72"

Twin Size: 72" x 90"

Queen Size: 90" x 90"

DON'T FENCE ME IN

Woodpile blocks surround rail fence blocks for a striking quilt.
Adjust border width if needed for a deeper mattress height.

CUTTING (lap, twin, queen, king)

FIRST CUT   **SECOND CUT**

Assorted Prints
cut (3, 4, 4, 6) strips 6½" x 21"
cut (3, 4, 4, 6) strips 5" x 21"
cut (3, 4, 4, 6) strips 3½" x 21"
cut (63, 124, 204, 366) strips 2" x 21"

Contrast
cut (8, 8, 10, 15) strips 2" x 42" . . . . cut (15, 15, 20, 30) 2" x 21"

Border
cut (7, 8, 10, 12) strips 7 ½" x 42" . . . . set aside for border
cut (2, 2, 2, 3) strips 6½" x 42" . . . . cut (3, 4, 4, 6) strips 6½" x 21"
cut (2, 2, 2, 3) strips 5" x 42" . . . . cut (3, 4, 4, 6) strips 5" x 21"
cut (2, 2, 2, 3) strips 3½" x 42" . . . . cut (3, 4, 4, 6) strips 3½" x 21"
cut (2, 2, 2, 3) strips 2" x 42" . . . . cut (3, 4, 4, 6) strips 2" x 21"

Binding
cut (7, 9, 10, 13) strips 2½" x 42" . . . . set aside for binding

YARDAGE (lap, twin, queen, king)

Assorted Prints
(12, 20, 29, 50) fat quarters (18" x 21")

Contrast
(⅝, ⅝, ¾, 1) yds.

Border
(2⅝, 2¾, 3¼, 4¼) yds.

Binding
(⅝, ¾, ⅞, 1) yds.

Backing
(3¾, 5½, 8, 11½) yds.

Quilt Sizes
Lap: 59" x 74"
Twin: 74" x 89"
Queen: 89" x 104"
King: 119" x 119"

SEWING (lap, twin, queen, king)

BEFORE YOU BEGIN: Test your seam allowance! If it is not exact, your blocks will not be square!

A. Stitch assorted print strips, background strips, and contrast strips into (3, 4, 4, 6) sets exactly as shown. Press all seams toward the contrast. Strip sets must measure 8" x 21". Cut each set into 2" units.

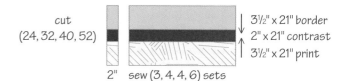
cut (24, 32, 40, 52)
3½" x 21" border / 2" x 21" contrast / 3½" x 21" print
sew (3, 4, 4, 6) sets

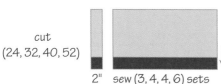
cut (24, 32, 40, 52)
6½" x 21" border / 2" x 21" contrast
sew (3, 4, 4, 6) sets

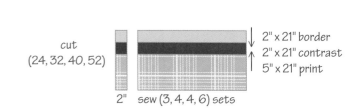
cut (24, 32, 40, 52)
2" x 21" border / 2" x 21" contrast / 5" x 21" print
sew (3, 4, 4, 6) sets

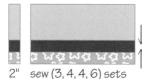
cut (24, 32, 40, 52)
5" x 21" border / 2" x 21" contrast / 2" x 21" print
sew (3, 4, 4, 6) sets

cut (24, 32, 40, 52)
2" x 21" contrast / 6½" x 21" print
sew (3, 4, 4, 6) sets

B. Stitch the step A units together to make blocks exactly as shown. Press. **Blocks must measure 8" x 8".**

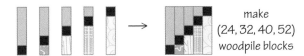

make
(24, 32, 40, 52)
woodpile blocks

C. Stitch assorted 2" x 21" strips together as shown in a variety of combinations. Press. **Strip sets must measure 8" x 21".** Cut into 8" blocks.

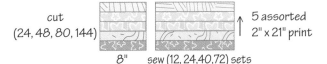

cut
(24, 48, 80, 144)

5 assorted
2" x 21" print

8"   sew (12, 24, 40, 72) sets

FINISHING

D. Arrange the **Step C** blocks exactly as shown, alternating the direction of the blocks, and making sure that the colors are evenly distributed. Do not sew them together yet!

Lap: center blocks set 4 x 6 (shown)
Twin: center blocks set 6 x 8
Queen: center blocks set 8 x 10
King: center blocks set 12 x 12

E. Arrange the **Step B** Woodpile blocks around the edges.

F. Stitch into rows as shown. Press in the direction shown by the arrows. Stitch the rows together and press.

G. Stitch 7½" x 42" border strips together as needed to make borders long enough for the quilt. Trim two borders to the exact width of the quilt and stitch to the top and bottom edges of the quilt. Press. Trim two borders to the exact length of the quilt and stitch to the sides. Press.

H. Layer and quilt by hand or machine. Bind using the 2½" x 42" strips.

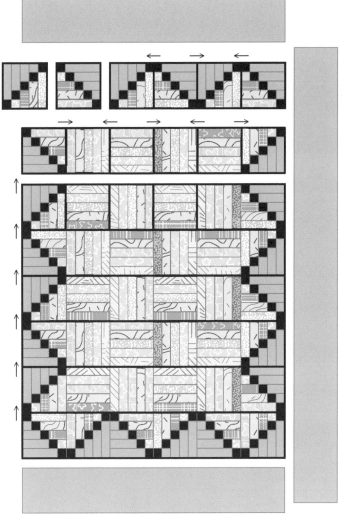

STARS ALL AROUND

This small quilt is shown on the back cover.

CUTTING

CENTER STAR
Follow the cutting instructions on page 6.

FLOATING STARS
Follow the cutting instructions on page 8 for the square size quilt. (12 stars)

CHECKED BORDER
Background
cut 6 strips 2" x 42"....... cut 11 - 2" x 21"

Assorted Prints
cut 11 strips 2" x 21"

BINDING
cut 5 strips 2½" x 42"

YARDAGE

Assorted Prints
7 fat quarters (18" x 21")
Scraps may be used for more variety.

Background 2 yds.

Backing 2¾ yds.

Binding ½ yd.

Quilt Size: 42" x 42"

SEWING

A. CENTER STAR: Follow the sewing instructions on page 6 to make the center star.

B. FLOATING STARS: Repeat Steps A - C on page 8 to make twelve star blocks.

C. Arrange the star blocks around the center star as shown. Stitch together into rows and press. Stitch the rows together. Press.

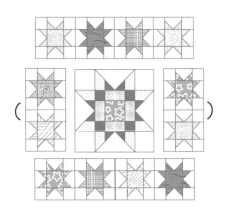

D. BORDER: Stitch 2" x 21" assorted print and background strips together as shown. Press. Cut into 2" units.

cut 104

2" sew 11 sets

↓ 2" x 21" background
2" x 21" print

E. Stitch 24 Step D units together as shown for the top and bottom borders. Adjust seams if needed so the borders are the exact width of the quilt. Stitch borders to the top and bottom edges of the quilt. Press.

Stitch 28 Step D units together as shown for the side borders. Adjust seams if needed so the borders are the exact length of the quilt. Stitch borders to the side edges of the quilt. Press.

F. Layer and quilt by hand or machine. Bind using the 2½" x 42" strips.

Monterrey Medallion, challenge version

Stars All Around

- use fat quarters for easy fabric selection
- quilt projects in three sizes
- choose the simple or challenge version
- arrange the blocks any way you'd like

Atkinson Designs
one of life's simple pleasures

ATK-602

6 43053 00602 7

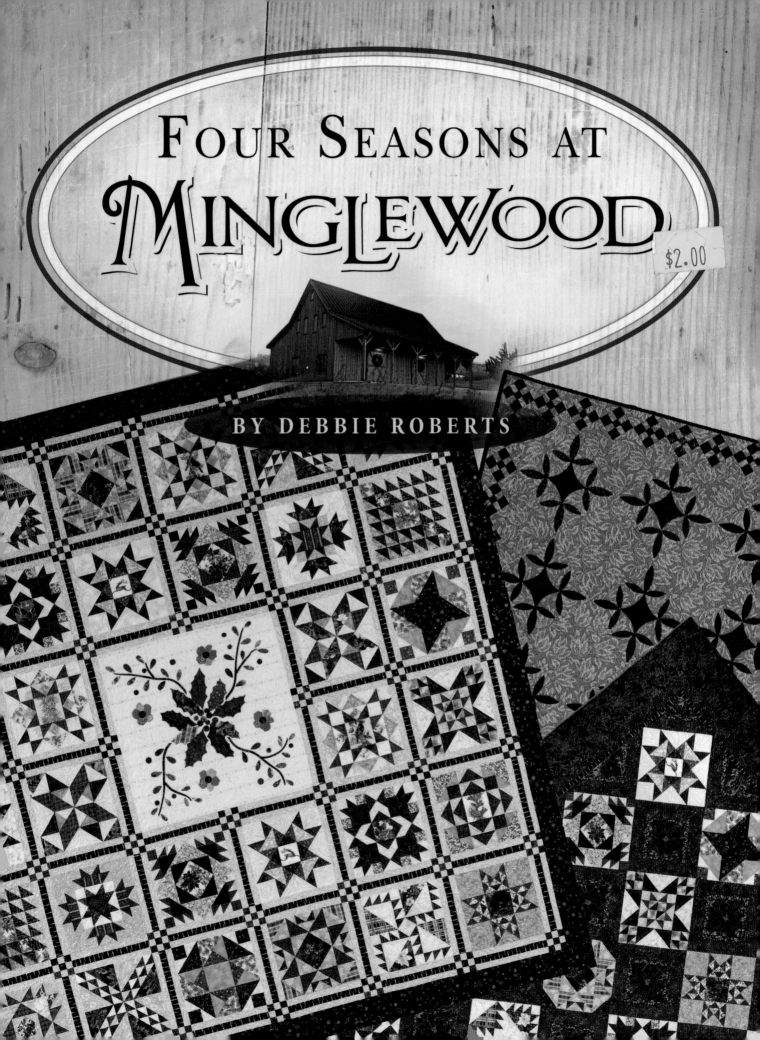

FOUR SEASONS AT MINGLEWOOD

BY DEBBIE ROBERTS